A Pot of Hot Milk

Philip James Kirke

Friend

BOOKS

First published 2012 by Friend Books

Copyright ©   1996 Philip James Kirke

National Library of Australia Cataloguing-in-Publication entry:

Author: Kirke, Philip James.

Title: A pot of hot milk

Edition: 1st ed.

ISBN: 978-0-9775243-5-8 (pbk)

Target Audience: For young adults.

Subjects: Family secrets--Juvenile fiction.

Dewey Number: A823.4

Friend

BOOKS

Friend Books   99 CORINTHIAN ROAD   WEST SHELLEY, WESTERN AUSTRALIA 6148

Dedication

To Catherine Gartner

with love

we met on the Matterhorn
became engaged on the slopes of Annapurna
and have made our home
on the banks of the Canning

The pursuit of beauty is always costly,

often dangerous,

and occasionally fatal

Chapter 1

Fractured Memory

The bathroom was a small yellow room off the back veranda. Midnight visits in winter were a cold affair, a dreaded necessity. And she had been unable to sleep. The face in the mirror was not old, but a first white hair or two, incongruous against her smooth skin, made her appear, well, less young. She breathed deeply and stared at her own eyes, as if at a daughter's eyes, trying to see the parent in the daughter. She couldn't sleep and she couldn't even figure out why. She stared, and as she stared, images of the day just gone started to replay before her eyes, and she watched passively. As a counsellor in the juvenile justice system disturbing days were not atypical. But today was different. Today something shifted.

She had been going through some old training videos, long forgotten, maybe never played since recorded. Maybe played to bored trainees, maybe for laughs, maybe dissected like a rat. A human trade.

The video had been black and white, and scratchy. The image jumped and re-set itself, and the voices were muffled, but the intensity of the encounter was plain enough, even with the passage of thirty years. The interview had been confusing, chaotic; none of the threads of the exchange seemed to link or lead anywhere. As she attempted to piece back its disturbing exchanges, she could recall only snatches, images which were particularly vivid and intense. The interviewee was barely out of adolescence, maybe nineteen, maybe twenty five, she couldn't tell.

"With your permission," the detention-centre interviewer had said, "we will be recording these sessions for use as training videos for trainee officers, OK?"

But the kid had shouted, his voice breaking into a desperate squeak, "No that's not OK! I'm not an exhibit!" He was not really a kid, a young man somewhere between teens and twenties, though not really either.

There was something in the poise of this almost-man, that defied definition. Rough looking yes, long dark matted hair, badly fitting clothes, big, dark, if not black: cotton and canvas. He had what appeared to be a rough scrap of rope tied around one wrist.

If she had to say, she would have said this child-man was gentle, shy, as if the entire world were an unfathomable mystery to him. Sometimes his gaze appeared fearless, the fearlessness of one to whom the entire earth is no longer of any importance; a fearlessness wrought from an existence that has exhausted all sources of loss, known too much too soon, for too long. But this was not the whole of it. His eyes seemed to suggest that he lived in, or for, some other -for want of a better word - "grace"; That he had given himself up entirely to it, what ever "it" may actually be. Occasionally, fleetingly, he seemed to smile, though it was the slightest nuance of the eyes, not the face.

But sometimes his gaze betrayed a horror that was beyond fear. The innocent horror of the abused.

This was the sense that hung about the man, intangible, unnameable, but real all the same.

The interviewer paused and spoke again, unruffled and perfectly polite, "You see; you are one of our most articulate "residents", and your case is, well, unusual. Please think about this. It could be of great benefit to others."

The boy glanced briefly directly to the camera, to the viewer, to Angela across thirty years. And as she looked into his eyes, through the years, she clearly saw fear. But she couldn't tell whether it was his fear she was seeing... or her own.

He must have noticed the video running, or something else must have occurred prior to the recording session, but whatever the reason, he turned on the interviewer suddenly "You fucking lied to me! You fucking lied!"

The interviewer's response was calm and practiced, "It's that language, that has landed you in the trouble you're in." It was if the meaning and context of the youth's speech was no longer of any consequence now that he, the interviewer, had some obvious offence against which to justify himself. To whom he felt he ought to justify himself, and the cost of that justification, were, it seemed, not ideas he had considered.

"My language? You fucking lied to me!"

Angela had frowned a little at this point. Something about the kid's mode of expression seemed to contradict his outwardly rough appearance, as if he were more educated than he would have others believe;

But perhaps it was the other way around, that this truly was man turned wild. Bizarrely a thought flashed across her mind of those strange "feral" children, raised by wild animals, discovered much later, irreparably wild. She watched on sceptically. There's no bigger pain in the arse than an earnest young man, she thought.

The kid leant forward, shaking, he raised his finger, his lips parted, but no words came out. His eyes seemed to drift off to one side, his hand dropped to his lap and, finally, he spoke quietly, but with a new tone, as if he had just thought of something,

"OK then.

I have my reasons. That's cool..."

Then, as an almost inaudible after-thought, "It will be worth recording your stupidity".

A strange smile played briefly on the interviewer's lips, somewhere between incredulity and a smirk. He clapped his hands together "Fine then, shall we make our way to the interview room?" He stood and gestured with a polite flourish of his hand. The kid stood and shuffled out, hunched, his arms now folded tightly across his chest.   Several other figures followed them from the room.

The image cut and then recommenced almost immediately, in a different room. The detention-centre interviewer, the kid and a couple of other figures sat in low chairs in a room devoid of human touch.

What was never clear to Angela, was whether this institution was a correctional facility, or a hospital, or some other. And it was never clear on what pretext the youth had been detained, and indeed whether his case were actually a matter of the justice system, or a medical one.   There are some cases that sit uncomfortably outside all the categories that society has erected, with which to sift, sort and accommodate its citizens.

As the interview progressed however, the actual offence committed by this man-child, if such were indeed the case, seemed to Angela to assume less importance, to her at least. Whatever he had said or done, it was emerging that it was really the boy's strangeness that had attracted the unwanted attention he was now getting. She watched on.

"You realise giving a false name was an offence don't you?" said the interviewer.

"I know who I am" said the youth sullenly.

"Where were you going when we picked you up?"

The image had jumped, blurred and disappeared completely for a full two minutes, though the sound continued, if scratchy and difficult to discern. The boy's voice was now low, contemplative, as if there were no one else in the room

"You been up the coast man?"

...silence...

"You drive for hours and the buildings and highways never thin out ay? There's no outer limit...

You never arrive at a city centre and you never leave.

You read of prophets going out into the wilderness. These days they would have to make do with the outer suburbs... That's all we have now.

The coast itself is hardly a transition to nature, more a hard line, a fracture where the city stops and the sea starts. The buildings come right to the water, some step down to it, stepping slowly down, below the surface, as if laying claim to the Ocean.

The sea seems violated, not so much a place of life now but a death, an end, ay.

Behind…Behind it, the city, the freeways crowd on one another over the coastal sand plain, highways woven madly over themselves, a tangle of construction...warp without weft…Ultimately meaningless.

There's an ancient fig tree growing through a crack in the concrete. An immense grey freeway overpass runs nearly directly over that tree. Its great roots heave upwards out from the reinforced concrete… Labour pains… Breaking waters… Breaking steel, stone, infinitely patient...

A violent, mute affront...

An insult not forgotten…

The first fracture of a mutual lie…

White lie, white as bones."

The voice stopped, the picture was still missing, and a hissing, crackling silence hung, for a moment. Then the boy's voice continued, even more quietly. Quietly, but with too much emotion,

"If blood is thicker than water, lies are thicker than blood."

An adult's voice spoke briefly, "Reese...", but the boy continued, as if trying to find his own thought, not so much answering the original question, but trying to discern the space which preceded the question, a basis.

"It's strange you know, that tree growing through those layers of the city, that crack in the pavement, like a crack in Reality itself. Like, like the world is just a seashell; sky is only paper thin, there's a lot more here besides this, but its outside......

You come to this giant concrete promontory, it's huge, painted blue, pale blue. The paint is peeling away like bark. A huge sea wall, tilting back, curved....Layers and layers of construction from different times long forgotten. Each new layer, each addition built on the last, without any ever being fully demolished, or completed. Architecture without author, no society claiming ownership, each inheriting it from the last, all building on it but none accepting blame for it, an ancient rounded, blue Babylon of incomplete and perpetually unrealised visions. Curved, towering, pale blue, it has barely any paint remaining.

There's something frightening about that structure, something... Horrific.

That prom, there's an evil wave that breaks onto it. It is so steep, so sudden, so sucky. So dangerous. When I surf that, it's like the world stops, and as you drop into the pit, a silence overtakes you, and you are in the exact centre of the turning universe. It's a dance, the whirling dance of the surfy. And the violence of the wave, the sea, the city, is beyond, outside your field of vision. Your concentration is intense, liquid speed, effortless motion. You are a point of perfect stillness, at the heart of the ocean. It is a gift."

The picture flickered back. The room in the tape fell silent, except for the tin cup hum of the video going around. The kid spoke again, " I got this girl friend, She says I got grace, She knows who I am ay, what I am."

"You gave a false name, a false identity. That's partly why you are back here again now," the interviewer prompted him. Then he added, in a lower voice, "You're not well. That's plain enough for anyone to see."

The boy replied, "You only see the noise.

You see the traffic every morning? In this city? The whole city is crawling like a carcass, but in the exact centre of the city, at its very heart, is the river, a silent empty pool, reflecting the sky so perfectly that you'd think the sky is itself reflecting that sacred stream. That the 'made' is the 'maker'." He laughed at their looks. He smiled and continued, "And every morning the city awakes, from sleep to agitation, without pausing to notice a space between the two. And the early morning freeway stream of coloured metal flows beside the placid river, a live rattling necklace"

The interviewer spoke at last, "Reese…"
The boy corrected him, "Rishy"…

"Reese - what do you intend to do if we release you again ?"

The boy held his gaze, "oh this time I'll quit … heh … this time … don't worry ... oh I'm done ... done "

His face was briefly shadowed by the faintest of scowls and his attention seemed to turn inwards again. In a tiny, quiet voice, almost like a girl's, he seemed to break into a rhythmic chant, or a song, barely audible. Though his eyes stared ahead, they were focussed on nobody in the room. They seemed fixed on a horizon. His soft face dropped, and his eyes widened, barely perceptibly. The expressions that played on his face were so quick in succession, so subtle as to be unnameable, yet still something had clearly passed before his vision. His look was one of sadness, horror, irredeemable loss. His girl-voice quietly sang:

" the thin white sandy line of the Southern Ocean Sea, stretches long and lonely far away from me… if

I take my leave today, would you notice that I've gone away?"

The others shuffled a little.

After a silence, another queer little chant, barely audible,

"when I woke up to this world of pain, I knew I didn't want to be here again...When I saw this world spinning anxiety, I knew the last thing that I wanted was society, I just want to be, empty as the sea, flowing nowhere, going nowhere ...alone."

An uncanny silence took command of the room.

One of the other adult staff present, possibly a doctor, scanned some notes in front of him, skipping over the words, saying, "You mentioned a..." He waved his hand, as if as a cue for the kid to pick up the story. The kid said nothing. "...You mentioned an experience… An unusual experience…" The adult's head turned slowly, slightly, from side to side, as he all the while watched the kid's face for a clue. The kid said nothing. The doctor laughed at the silence, and at himself and then spoke, though it seemed really that he was thinking aloud, perhaps even in self criticism, "You know, the whole of modern psychiatric medicine is based on the twin pillars of Manic Depression and Schizophrenia. Perhaps, after all, our science is simply not holistic enough. Then he smiled at the boy, more with his eyes than his whole face, a first genuine offering of human kindness. It was more an apologetic appeal than a smile. It seemed as if he might almost, almost - mind, be beginning to understand the boy's countenance, his desperation, and his intelligence, which the first interviewer had, in his own way, already acknowledged. He checked his notes quietly. The man-child and the others were silent.

A third interviewer looked intently at the kid and spoke for the first time. She was younger than the men present. She had short lightish hair, freckles. She sat closest to the boy. Her tone was like a question, though hushed, even awed, barely more than a whisper. Her eyes had abandoned all professional distance, all medical aloofness and six years of Medical training at University: "It was real? Then why are you so distressed?"

The child spoke quietly, acknowledging this last interviewer's own dignity, but barely whispering his answer... "because I can't tell anyone...ever..."

After a long silence, the three institution staff leaned ever so slightly towards each other and engaged in what appeared to be intense hushed argument. Then, without warning, the initial interviewer strode towards the camera and turned it off. The tape cut again.

When it resumed, the first interviewer was saying simply, "Reese Carnegie we will be recommending you for discharge. Perhaps it was a mistake that you were brought here ... perhaps".

The boy spoke, " My name is not Reese, it is Rishy".

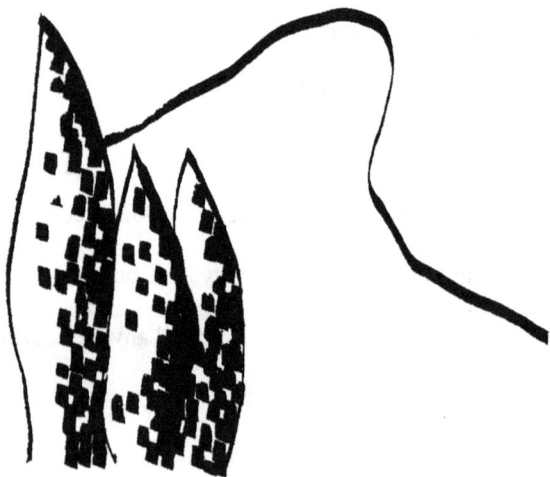

Chapter 2

The Frame

Angela turned distractedly away from the bathroom mirror and turned to step outside in to the cold midwinter air, forgetting why she had gone to the bathroom in the first place. As she turned to go back into the house, she paused on the sagging planks of the veranda, and then suddenly, for no reason at all, she stepped off the planks into the crisp cold grass and walked between tangled roses and vegetables towards the bottom of the garden instead. She arrived at the stand of eucalypts at the back of the garden. The black canopy of the trees, framed a patch of the night sky, a rocking, rustling leafy frame and a silent, violent sky. And beyond the trees' leafy frame, the restless cloudscape formed a window which itself framed a patch of brilliant white stars. The full moon raced across the shifting skyscape of clouds, blinking, staring, racing, as vast worlds, complete and complex, formed and faded in the rippled cloudscape. No memory, no ruins, no manuscripts recorded each perfect cloud scene before it was erased, like a civilisation. The high tide of her memory receded, and the moist, stony sea-bed of the past revealed itself, unexpected, uninvited and in startling clarity and accuracy. The years parted, and she remembered.

She herself had never had children, but she sometimes watched the children of others, and mused wryly how children simply seemed to be brain-damaged adults. And childhood, the process of becoming adult, seemed to her little better than a protracted, unguarded opportunity for damage, a period of intolerable and outrageous vulnerability. But if the purpose of childhood was simply to become adult, she wondered, what then followed adulthood?

She remembered her sister. When their father had failed to return that awful day, it was as if the bond that bound them also broke. A sacred thread that bound the three of them had snapped, and all three beads had scattered. Without the three, there was none. The trinity was a unity, or nothing at all. Some say that adversity unites, and though some truth may be found in this, it is equally true that too severe an adversity drives souls irreparably apart, where once they were bound by love.

She remembered her father, fabulous and flawed. Men are a strange kind of woman, she mused; at best: pillars of strength, but always complicated bundles of contradictions. Nothing about them is permanent, reliable or true. Though their hearts, some of them, may be good. Her father had delighted in telling stories to her and to her sister. He had an uncanny knack of entering their world and acknowledging the reality of their fantasy and imagination, as if nothing were more ordinary. The shallow hill on which their small family home perched became a Himalayan mountain, the stand of eucalypts: a forest, individual days became whole years, and their father's daily absence at work, became a parting and a journey of great duration that all of them dreaded, a separation that each felt acutely, and wished it didn't have to be that way. And often their father spoke to them in earnest, in a quiet voice that was urgent and precise. He would speak to them of matters most real, most serious, but in their own language, a language of imaginings, where reality and fantasy merged and danced. And it seemed to Angela and to her sister that their father were entrusting them with secrets he wouldn't share with other adults, that only they might understand, and that even they might not. It is frightening sometimes to remember the past clearly, to see in video replay events which we had convinced ourselves to forget because they were too beautiful, too real, too undeniable. We forget in order to dull the pain of beauty lost, to comfort ourselves with the lie that what was lost was never ours anyway, that we had misunderstood those cherished moments, that they were mere projections and were not real. Sudden lucid memory denies us that comfort, and the pain and the beauty that come flooding back, are both exquisite. Her father had once said that the pursuit of beauty is always costly, often dangerous, and occasionally fatal. She remembered her father's last story and her body prickled with emotion, the garden blurred, and the night poured over her head like oil.

Chapter 3

A Pot of Hot Milk

Oh my two daughters.

I have become drunk on your sweet laughter.

My head is spinning like your painted wooden spinning-top. Bright yellow and red designs have flooded my weary mind with colours and the purple night has exhaled deeply, a sigh of countless stars and breezes tinged with distant melodies. I cannot stop giggling myself. Stop it now. No more silly jokes. You are too beautiful for this night. I am blessed indeed to be your father. Come outside my sweet daughters, come out onto the roof and let us enjoy the warm mountain breezes. The forests are calling us outside, this night, as if with much to tell and joy to share. Come outside onto the thick oak planks which have been the faithful witness to all your childhood games, and all my blessed four years as your father, your friend in this vast world. Your eyes are sweet, wide and pure like those of your mother on the night you were conceived. Come outside, these rough white walls can contain me no longer this night. Will you share a quiet hour with me now by the low wooden balcony, deep in the sighing night air, and let us see what the night is waiting patiently to tell us.

Yes, it is more pleasant out here is it not? The countless forest leaves are rustling on all sides, like the silken threads of a woven coat, each thread more colourful than its weaving neighbour, gold penetrating purple, the darkest blue spun like a stream amongst the darkest greens.

Am I sad? Yes perhaps I am sad. My sadness has called me from our long finished meal and my heart is filling with new thoughts like the fathomless pond by the midnight waterfall. My four years with you both has been a joy and my heart's fulfilment. Yet you cannot know how it is to miss your mother for she left as you arrived. You have known your mother only as the snug warm liquid home you shared for the nine months of your twin-hood. The Autumn leaves are scattered. She is gone and shall not reform on the returning breeze. A family we are and I your mother and father both.

Behold you have both become silent. Your mere four years have become an ageless nobility. You wish to know my thoughts. Have I not told you during our dinner earlier on this evening? I am going away. My business has called me away. For the life of a man rides the returning tide and is not apart from it. And now that month is dawning that my work again beckons my descent from these mountain valleys. It has been so long since I last went that perhaps you two cannot recall. But it has always been thus. A man's home is but his resting place and not his permanent abode. Yet I shall return here as the osprey does to his nest, and we shall laugh again.

I hope.

Yes perhaps I feel apprehension. 'Tis a long descent to the sea and her evil smelling ports. 'Tis a deeper descent to the secret oyster beds in which I work. And 'tis a deeper descent still should my nerve fail me and I slip into the blackness of the 'drop-off'. I have gazed on occasions during my work down to that black depth and have wondered what lies further down. You can see only the last tumbling gouges of rock as the ledge turns like an eddying waterfall and plummets away. I dread the drop-off. I have seen shadows of sharks flicker in the corner of my eye, barely visible enough to be certain, barely ambiguous enough to offer the comfort of any alternative explanation. My work is poised on a narrow shelf amongst the flickering fishes, prising and probing the sleeping oysters to locate that rare fellow who may be harbouring that tiny and valuable white tumour. You have sometimes asked me whether the little shell-dwelling animal is hurt by my work, but I tell you again, he is relieved and grateful that I remove the growing source of his irritation. And for my part, the value of one single pearl justifies my work for that time and is the signal that I may return to you both away up here, where a man belongs, with his daughters in the good warm air of these forested slopes.

Look upon the spinning stars and the strange luminous white slopes that lean toward the sky. You have asked me to describe the inner light with which a pearl seems to glow. 'Tis like that snow in the starlight. It is soft and delicate, rich and fathomless. It is white like the seamless breaking of the waves upon the shore, I refer to the sound of the breaking waves, not their appearance. But you have not heard the waves of the sea and so my words perhaps mean nothing. Then it is like the light of the throbbing waterfall as you lie amongst the ancient tangled roots of the trees at the bottom of the forest pool and gaze upwards at the endless white fall above. Do you remember that night we all held hands and lay directly beneath the waterfall's foot, in the bottom of the deep pool. We gazed upwards and held our breaths, humming the tune Angelica always hums when she is in a good mood. You know the one Satyina? A pearl is white and glows with the light of that midnight waterfall, and all its millions of tiny bubbles.

My work is hard and I dread each time the return of its call. But the time has again called. When tomorrow has dawned and you both awaken in your big bouncy bed, I will have gone, and you shall not see me for a time. If I could write I would, but no one comes to these forested peaks and there is no one to deliver a letter. Be patient and await my return and I will be wealthy again for a time, and shall remain a long while with you both. I hope you shall not be so very much older when I return. I miss you terribly as I toil in the cold currents of the heaving sea.

My two sweet girls. I do not wish to leave you with advice. For you will learn only that which your heart seeks to know and truly I have gained more from the flash of your clear-pool eyes than you shall ever learn from my stumbling words. But as this night drains from our hands like the beach sand, I find tales and stories swimming in my heart, that seek to be shared. And if I offer to you what my heart desires to give, in love, and in love only, then perhaps there is no harm in my speech. For as you have shared with me your beauty and your laughter, perhaps I may share what is mine though much of it may be sadness and weariness. For my sadness is true and perhaps it may claim a value by virtue of its hard-won authenticity.

And as a ragged jewel, broken from the baked rock of a desert hill is valuable and beautiful, perhaps my weary tales may be worth something. For I offer, through them, the purity of my heart.

I am not an old man. Indeed I am a young man, not even three decades are mine, Yet I hold that I am qualified to speak. For even old men are not really old. Not really. They stoop and they grumble as if to appear old. But they are not old. I came upon a ragged, moss-cloaked tree in an ancient forest on an island near Antarctica. That tree was two thousand years old and showed no signs of stooping. Old men seek to snatch our respect by feigning age. They are not old. So I shall speak.

But I shall also listen. I shall listen to your far-flung youth as I share this evening's shelter with you both. Your lives are a splash of colours. They have come

out of a single white and white came from black.
Who can explain this mystery? Let mysteries look
after themselves. Our brief lives, though brief, are
never-the-less worthwhile, and are measured in love.

A half hour of silence. Poured from the heart of the
night like wine from a bottle.

We gaze in idle harmony upon the mysterious
mountain slopes we three know and love so deeply.
Our breaths, all three, rise and fall in syncopated
tenderness. Your tiny lungs taste the mountain air as
if for the first time, and mine: as if for the last.

Perhaps.

Who knows. If a moment of love shared is preserved
in the memory of eternity, then perhaps its brevity is
an illusion, and love's intimate gifts are ours for ever.
If those passing moments which we would preserve

and clutch to our chest against all the storms of this world, seem impossible to retain, then perhaps we should let them pass, and in their passing, take a longer, fonder look and let the bliss of acceptance replace the struggle of craving.

I have known love. I have known love's passing and love's returning. And in its ceaseless wandering, perhaps love is ever with us after all, like the mountain stream. We know where to find the stream, and she flows with patient certainty, without fear of vanishing. Yet how often has it been said that the river is never the same, and what you gaze at one moment is not what you gaze upon the next.

Let me hold your tiny hands. For all the wise words in the world I would hold you two only, and this hour for ever. I grieve its passing.

Tonight I would tell you of things I have done, and of things which have befallen me. I would tell of battles I have fought against evil and ignorant men. I would tell of an evil grey dog that followed me in the shadows of the night, sometimes boldly even in the day forever seeking to take my throat. I would tell of a man who is (I can think of no other description) a hole in the sky. When he walks a great peace and majesty surrounds him, and I tremble in love at his beauty and power. I would tell of some desert people who cast magic upon the grey dog and freed me of its shadow. I would tell of a strange place I discovered where these mountains end, and the sky begins, and the echo of your voice precedes your voice itself, that your voice becomes the echo of a vaster music and you find yourself sitting upon every mountain in this range at once. Tonight I would tell you of the things my heart has never told, and it shall be my privilege and indulgence to share these things for the very first time.

But first, let us make a pot of hot milk. The evening

is   becoming   cool.

Chapter 4

An Architect

$\mathcal{M}$y daughters.

When I was your age I would follow my Great Great Grandmother about in her berry garden. She kept a garden in which would grow every kind of berry. There were strawberries and hayberries. There were blueberries and greenberries. There were mulberries, blackberries, cherry trees and berry-berries. And as she tended the wild and colourful tangle of sweetness in the golden sun, I would follow her and chatter. She would say I was terrible chatterbox. But she said it with the love of a mother. She was a grand mother. She was a great mother. And once, not long after I had become aware of the mystery of Work, I began to wonder aloud in what manner of Work I would engage when I became big like my father. She laughed and said "You will become a philosopher"

"What is a philosopher" I asked her. She tried to explain it to me but it all sounded a bit odd and I did not understand what she was saying. Finally she said "Oh he is one who dives for pearls" and dismissed the subject from further discussion.

Once, when I pursued the subject of my future Work with particular vigour, my Great Great Grandmother paused long enough to take me seriously for a moment and suggested, "Perhaps you could be a good Architect. For you are always making things and an Architect is a respected Profession. You could make tables and chairs and houses and cabinets".

I was horrified. Our house already had many chairs. Chairs and chairs. The floor was not wasted as it spread like a puddle on the bathroom tiles. It was all well settled with chairs, flat-lapped and empty. I sulked and considered once again the feasibility of becoming a philosopher.

My daughters. Let me demonstrate for you how I prepare for Work. For it is a ritual which is becoming for one who knows the inseparable role that it must play in our lives. Follow me now to my small white room with the honey-golden wooden floor boards.

See this is my cloak, it is woven loosely and roughly of raw hessian. I remove my shoes, for one does not wear shoes to work. That would be irreverent. My indigo pants are fine, they are loose and comfortable, and the dark indigo blue is a splendid colour. And this is my hessian cloak. It must be worn in exactly the right manner, and a man is recognised from afar as A Man Going About His Work if he has worn his hessian cloak in the right manner. You see you drape its heavy folds about your shoulders like this, and bunch it up about your neck. Then, (watch carefully): you fold the right hand side over the left shoulder like this and wrap the left hand side around the waist like this. Then you crinkle this bit, and rimple this bit.

Finally you tuck the edge of the left hand bit under the folds made by the right hand bit....like so! And now... I am ready for work! Yes to build houses and their furniture, No! Not any more. For no longer am I an Architect. Now I am A Deep Sea Oyster Surgeon, and tomorrow I...

Yes Satyina, I suppose I am sad. Come, it is still the night before the morning after the day which precedes the day of departure. Here, I'll remove this ridiculous cloak, and we'll sit together on the fourth balcony, the one curved like a piano, and I'll tell you more of my tale.

See these balconies, how they ascend the Living Hall of our rough white house? Each balcony is of a different timber, each of a different hue, each warm with either an Autumn Gold or Red, or a Ruby Brown or a Tawny Orange that tells of the warmth of the heart of the tree. Each comes from a different tree, and each tree came from a different Continent. For our house, though small, owes its entirety to the joyful union of its parts, which have converged to give us shelter from the nine corners of the Earth. And indeed though many may claim that they owe nothing to the wealth of far-off lands, there has not been a time that the patient winds have not carried the ships of men from one land to another, providing things we eventually come to regard as our own. The worst men are those who acknowledge no debt and pay no tribute to those lands which they have never seen, and perhaps never even heard of, yet which are the authors of the very fabric of their bones.

See how brightly polished are these finely turned balconies? Notice this delicate double turn at the edge? See these fine rosewood blades, curved like the wing of an Osprey? This is the work of my hands. This is the work of an Architect. For at the time it seemed to me that a house is but a larger item of furniture, and should be made in the very same way, to be touched, and to be as comfortable. See our family mirror, down there in the hall. See how the tall black rectangle shines with the perfect image of all that passes before it. I polished that ebony slab until I could see the past, present and future, in its liquid sheen. It may seem unlikely to you, but some houses of men have mirrors made of silvered glass. We, being poor, could afford no such luxury and have had to make do with African Ebony.

And when I was of the age, the old men of the surrounding tribes came to our family home and took me away to be taught the Things Which Are Known. It didn't take long because Men know so very little, but still we must teach and be taught. And it was agreed that I should become An Architect and I was put on a ship and sent away to a very good teacher. By some probably insignificant coincidence, his name was the same as mine. Though this is not remarkable as it is a common enough name...in some circles. I remember the day I departed on that ship. The white ship cut across the black water, with its flaky, layered surface, each melting, crumbling fragment of water grasping the white sunshine. The air was cold, the islands stationary, though they gave the impression of jostling for position as the boat spun a slow arc around on its way. I could feel the rise and fall of the nonchalant boat. A broad timber rail spun around the front of a high deck. (I think sailors call it the "Bridge"). The smooth, polished rail was warm, rich in its forest colour, intricately grained like the layered songs of the forest birds who once fought upon its branches. My brother before me, who was to become a Weaver of Curtains, had been sent to Curtain University. I was sent to the School of the Makers of Architecture.

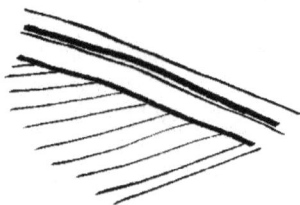

Chapter 5

Forbidden Explorations

$\mathcal{L}$ isten !

Listen! Do you hear that? What a noise! All the night birds have burst into song. Have you ever heard such singing? Such whistling, chirping, squeaking and tooting. I have only ever heard such bird song in the hour immediately before the dawn. That hour before the sun appears, the birds seem to know and they burst forth in an eerie, otherworldly opera, before you are quite free of your dreams. And it seems somehow unreal, or more real than anything else you have known. Such life! And there is no moon tonight. Only stars. It is as if the stars themselves are so bright that that alone is sufficient excuse to burst into song. The sun is not needed. Just the stars. What singing.

Beautiful.

Sit close to me my sweet children. One on either side, in the floppy folds of my jumper. Let me feel my heavy arms about your shoulders as I tell you more of my tale.

My studies. Yes. I journeyed to the Land of the Etruscans. For that is where my Teacher lived and indeed the Land of the Etruscans boasted some of the finest of the arts of all sorts, not least of which was that of Architecture. And so, in the stone cloisters and workshops of the School of the Makers of Architecture, I began to learn all the skills of my trade. It was a fun class of young men and women, and some of the women were very pretty.

We were taught the nature of materials, wood of course, but also stone, twine, and the newly discovered copper, which you two can see down there in the vast pan hanging on the wall, and the water pot beside it. We learned how to square a log, and plane it to a true and faultless surface. We learned how to join two pieces with tenon and mortise so that the two became as one, and never parted. No nails or glue are needed. We were taught the relative strengths and properties of all these good materials. We learned to turn wood on a lathe and clay on a wheel. We learned the correct and sensible way to use every fine thing, and how to assemble shelves and tables, chairs and desks, stools and beds and benches and racks for keeping things on. I quickly excelled in the practical skills.

Until one day.

A new girl had joined the class. Something about her caught my fascination.

The New Girl had eyes like stones, brightly polished to an exquisite life.

I was hypnotised by her. I couldn't stop staring. One day she spoke to me, "Are you coming to the new classes?"

"What new classes?" I asked, unable to say more.

She smiled gently...She knew. "Beauty" she said quietly.

A visiting Teacher had been invited to teach us the ways of Beauty. He sat amongst us on the leather hide rugs and spread out parchment drawings of pieces of work he had seen both in the Land of the Etruscans and far to the East in Lands I had not even heard of.

The black ink-line images captivated me. A whole new world opened before me. For the pieces he showed us were no less useful than the robust objects we had been making, and no less well built. Indeed, many had been assembled with a far finer understanding of the mysteries of balance and inner strength of materials. But that is not all. They had a grace and a slenderness. They had a turn of curve and a tilt of plane. They had a rhythm in their parts and a strange sense of purpose that went far beyond the most obvious reasons for their conception. It would be true to say that the entire class quickly came to prefer these lessons to any other.

But to me, an ambition had been ignited. I wanted to create the most beautiful pieces that would ever appear on this Earth. I wished to create pieces so beautiful that people would cry in awe that such beauty could exist. I wanted to move people with the same sense of mystery and wonder that was beginning to dawn in my heart. Because, of all the things I had beheld in my short life, nothing else now seemed so significant. And so late one night when almost everyone was asleep in their beds, I gave my pet osprey to a friend to look after and I left the School, vowing not to return until I had unlocked the secret of beauty. For the visiting teacher had shown inspiring images but his explanations of what these things were and why they appeared as they did, were unconvincing. Of their beauty all agreed. None was in doubt. And the saying that beauty is only in the eye of the beholder had never seemed so ignorant; we were unanimous as to their charm and grace. It was the shallow explanations that left me unconvinced. If the best teachers in the land had no answers, then I must find them for myself!

So I set off, with a bottle of red wine wrapped in an olive green cloth, a flute and half a loaf of tomorrow's bread, surreptitiously given to me by the School Baker with a wink as I entered, and a quizzical frown as I turned to leave. He knew my purpose but could not understand my reasons.

I came to the City On Seven Hills, and wandered a while in the busy streets. On the first evening, a swarm of swallows swallowed the sky, seething black above the seething black streets.

I watched the twisting oil-on-water patterns, swelling and collapsing like a lung, flickering so that they seemed not like black flecks on the evening-white sky, but as a shimmering white light on a black background. I suddenly saw how the *appearance* of things has a reality all of its *own*, quite unrelated to the reality of the objects that generate it!

I journeyed on to a place known as Verona, by a river. I wandered the streets gazing at all that met my eyes, with a loose and relaxed mind, asking myself, "Is this beautiful? Is this beautiful? Why? Why? Why?" Finally, weary and no wiser, I sat down in the piazza in the centre of the town and gazed absently at the passing scene.

There were many milling people, spilling and swilling, like water in a tub. Black coats, stockinged legs, rattling tongues, and feet swinging like pendulums, across the broad pavement, from left to right, through and across, cutting great arcing lines, invisible paths of purpose, from house to work or vice versa, each carrying a lifetime of ideas, worries, frustrations and unanswered questions. They moved, cupped between gold and apricot apartments.

I felt alone. Everybody was too busy or distracted to care about the thing that was aching in my heart.

I journeyed on to the City on the Water. I had heard it said that the City on the Water is a dead city, little more than an over-visited cliché. Well. I tend to think this new saying, parched in its spiralling cynicism, is the real cliché. Sure there is Death in the City on the Water: I saw a funeral there my first morning. A warm mumbling crowd had gathered at the great doors of their family church. The green waves lapped kindly on the descending steps behind them. The winter sun was unusually warm and humming boats passed back and forth through the wonderful discord of church bells each singing from a different campanile like birds from morning trees. The hearse was a boat, rising and dipping on the familiar waves. It carried a spent person and a bulging stack of bright flowers, red, yellow and pink, across the blue water. The city smiled in similar colours. Yes there is Death in the City on the Water....But how beautiful! Every city coughs a little and returns gradually to the dust and earth, but so few with the class and style of the City on the Water.

I wandered the alleys and canals of this place for days, often forgetting my quest as I was so absorbed in all that lay about me. I sat one lunchtime, in a residential district, munching on some cheese. A dirty little grumbling boat, laden low with roof tiles rumbled past, carting its orange load across the green water. Old brick houses, broken and full of windows waited calmly each day for returning residents. Bright paint here and crumbled stone there, flapping with laundry and darting with swallows, cut white and green down the middle by the well used canal. Pigeons alighted, on shaking feathered wings, plying meals from pavement cracks. Seagulls spiralled and complained. Men strode in discussion and children wandered in a thousand aimless tasks, marbles and names and inaudible jokes.

A bright boat, with a green deck, blue gunnels and lined with red, permanently bright with its temporary costume of timbered paint, leaned and shook, out and back from its tethering poles. One day, I thought, it will sail on secret purposes with its secret owner.

Elsewhere, a stranded gondolier, left high and dry, as the tourist tide abated (it was mid-winter) strutted and paraded, in his flat-top red-ribboned hat, greedily eyeing the pigeons for a tourist. I watched the shifting mass of feathered pigeons, as the Etruscans threw bread-crumbs, and tourists threw glances. The clanging of the bell in the tall brick campanile didn't alter the crazy dance: grey pigeons, red bricks and variously feathered people, in nylon and furs, laughing and discussing in that purring chortle, the Etruscan language.

I journeyed beyond the Land of the Etruscans, always asking myself what I felt about what I saw, going deeper and deeper into my own perceptions and feelings. I invented new words for the sensations that unfolded before me. I took nothing for granted and accepted everything that came before me.

I would watch an object of particular interest. I would note what I saw and also my reactions to it, what ever they may be. It may have been delight, or boredom, attraction or revulsion, curiosity or confusion, fear, amusement, and sensations which don't even have names, except for the names I gave them. And there were many far more subtle variations. I compiled notes and drew diagrams. Insane diagrams that no-one would understand. Even I didn't understand my own diagrams, but that didn't stop me.

And I journeyed on. I journeyed where ever my fancy took me. I journeyed as my evolving ideas led me. After many months I found myself in the mountains, not these mountains, but mountains not unlike these.

The grey mass was like an ultimatum, a challenge to realise my objective once and for all. As I stared at the layered depth of the heaving, folded wilderness, I felt a new thrill, of fear and of anticipation. I felt immense excitement at the possibilities that lay before me.

One grey evening a moist white sea of cloud swept silently over the peaks, all but obscuring the range. As it grew darker, the outlines grew more tenuous, and a sense of mystery overtook me. I gazed expectantly up into the white cloud, as night started to spread.

"Elusive Vision", I thought, "I have seen you, I have held you in my hand, I have caught rain-drop notes of your beauty; tight, taut, caught and held, you disappear behind white mist cloud like a rock peak, but appear, again and again. Vision of Joy; I'll find you and we'll dance, that impossible dance."

The next day as I ascended the peaks, I was tired, exhausted, thirsty and hot. I picked my way over the scattered grey boulders as I ascended the increasingly barren slopes. My head started to swim and I kept closing my eyes, trying to retain my balance. Setting my sights on a razor sharp stone ridge above and ahead, I forced myself to pick one foot after the other.

As I finally reached the stone spine I reached up with my left hand and heaved myself up. I stopped in sudden silence. Just over the ridge was a magnificent valley, not wide, not deep, indeed barely one thousand paces across. It was surrounded on all sides by the angry grey rock. But the valley itself was a picture of sweetness. Broad shady trees lay a cool blanket of dark green shade all about. A broad fast flowing river eddied and swirled, its pure water the perfect antidote to every thirst that ever was.

But before I could scramble down to sate my thirst and seek shelter from the heat I was struck by a realisation: the delight I found in this scene had nothing to do with the optics of seeing, or the mechanisms of image forming. This was a beauty quite different in its effect to the perceptual tease of the flickering light display of swallows I had stared at in awe, all those months ago. This was a beauty purely and completely of *meaning*, of *interpretation*, of *extrapolation* of the *significance* placed on the objects and their assemblage, that lay before me. The trees were beautiful, not because of any tantalising display of light, but crudely and simply because of the ample shade they offered. The river was beautiful, and not threatening, only because of my present thirst. The entire illusion of beauty was a hallucination generated from my particular needs of the time. I was staggered. If I was to tease the mystery of beauty from the things of this world I was going to have to delve deeper into the complete process of seeing, that began with the light and visual signals, inert and meaningless, and follow it through the physiological process of forming an image, and then the mental process of interpreting the implied significance of the information contained within the image.

It appeared that a significant response to beauty could be attributed to any or several of these stages and was not the exclusive property of any one of them. Further I delved until I perceived that the process of seeing, and interpreting, was a physical continuity with the objects seen; one undifferentiated continuity, and that the viewers' position within all this was a small part in the entire process.

The implied *meaning* beyond the reality of the scene or object beheld may be interpreted as "good" or "bad" depending on the inner needs and desires of an individual at a given point in time.

But so too the actual *process* of seeing and of interpreting had a reality of its own. For example, a complicated object may defy comprehension and cause difficulty of interpretation. This *object* does not convey any bad meaning of its own, but the interpretation *process* is thwarted by the complexity. The simple inability to interpret alone gives rise to a negative response.

Slowly, the idea of "Order" started to find a logical place in the scheme of things. Order, or the patterned organisation of form, did not guarantee beauty; it may indeed render the impression monotonous. But of course, so often order, of one sort or another, does indeed render the most exquisite and beautiful of responses. Why?

There seems to be at least three quite different reasons.

Order assists the *process* of seeing and assembling a comprehensible intelligible image, so that the perceptual process is assisted and the interest (as well as ease) contributed is pleasurable.

However, the implied *meanings* also of various forms of order (and there may be many) are often themselves of an agreeable nature.

But thirdly, order establishes a "ground" or "reference" against which *deviations* from that order may be recognised, gauged and interpretations drawn. Indeed order becomes a benchmark from which recognisable variations begin to imply stories, meanings of any manner. And it is these very *breaches of order* that contain the core of the deepest emotional responses arising from aesthetic perception of form, and I might add.....Music. And as your creative eyes and heart are honed, it becomes possible to become the author of meanings so subtle and so barely perceptible, that great symphonies of emotion may be played with a deft touch, all on account of an understanding of what meanings (however abstract), are likely to be drawn from any particular variation to an established order. And the type of ordering system plays as significant a role in this as the type, and extent, of breach to the order.

From this point I developed an entirely new science of perception to trace and structure of these perceptual processes.

Now all this is very well, but you have no idea what it means to totally consume yourself in such inward observation. Many times I feared I was crossing into the realms of mad-men. For this search occupied years and became a nightly pattern whereby the impressions of the day were gathered and studied for all hours of the night. I kept stacks and stacks of notes. Enormous quantities.

Then...

One night.......

As I sat upon a warm rocky ledge, with the idle
summer air carrying wisps of cloud about my feet,
and the moon and stars playing hide and seek, an
awful and stunning revelation struck me:

I had seen the start of perception in the events of the world, and their light-conveyed message to the eye. I had seen the eyes' reaction to the light-message and the message carried to the mind. I had seen the mind turn and respond, forming a comprehensible idea about what it saw, and then complex webs of implied meaning. I had seen the emotional response to these arise, be it beauty or any other. I had seen the whole process as one seamless continuity flowing and eddying. It was neither wholly inside my body, nor outside. Indeed the defined edge of where "I" began and left off suddenly became decidedly undefined. There was a process, the complete path of which I could trace and witness. But there was no "I". There was no particular place in which "I" resided! The whole purposeless machine turned without a "me". What I thought had been my very Heart was not my own at all. It did not in fact even exist.

Beauty and the very songs of the soul were nothing more than the ripples of a relentless, meaningless process; a beginning-less and endless cycle, like the tides and like the tired turning of a sleepless earth, restless, inevitable, predictable, impersonal and without respite.

I was dumb-founded. I had formulated myself out of existence! I could watch the whole inescapable nightmare, but still I did not even exist.

Now many mystics before me have speculated upon the non-identity of "I" with the body, but had anyone come so intimately and in such detail to those most intimate of processes with which we identify, the responses of the heart, the recognition of beauty, the most intimate and inner and personal responses which we call our own self? Who knows, but I had come face to face with the realisation that no depth, no matter how deep, or subtle, or personal was separate, sanctified, our own, apart from the entirety of the Universe. The existence of each of us as individuals appeared to be utter illusion. The Whole was One. And "*I*" was not *any* of it.

Or perhaps *all* of it?

I was shaken to my bones. For these were no mere speculations. These had been actual experiences, of great depth, and over a long period of time.

I sensed I had stumbled across uncharted territory of potentially awesome consequences if the knowledge was to be developed further and its ramifications understood. I felt I had discovered the next Atom Bomb, and an awesome responsibility went with it. I prayed to the Spirit of the Earth to take me under her wing. I had flirted with madness and discovered worlds within worlds. I was no longer sure of my way back. I lay down after my prayer to the Earth and fell into a deep sleep. When I awoke several hours later, my heart was flooded with a deep peace, and though I still felt fragile, an inner confidence and peace told me that the Earth had accepted my prayer.

What a strange turn things had taken! Here was I, sent off to learn to make Architecture, and I was now living and wandering alone in barren, unknown mountains, going mad in my self-imposed quest for the secret of beauty.

I spent one more month in this place, but was constantly dizzy and short of breath. The sun was fierce during the day and the nights were desperately cold. I had wandered into these mountains without any real intention of doing so, and it proved to be no place for man to live. The air was thin, and such small fish as I could catch in the streams were not much sustenance. So I left.

Picking my way back down the mountain slopes I felt weary and exhausted. I didn't feel any closer to my original goal, and I was no longer even enthusiastic for my quest for the secret of beauty. Further more I had not completed my studies at the School of the Makers of Architecture. I felt silly and confused. Deep inside myself, I knew I had discovered important secrets, but with every new discovery, I only realised how many more mysteries lay unsolved, and probably insoluble. And I felt that even the little I had started to understand had really no value at all unless it could be translated into reality. That is to say, until I had created pieces of work that shimmered in the imagination and stirred deep beautiful dream-world responses in the souls of people, I had not really attained anything. Any fool can postulate and write books. How few can distil symphonies from the black and silent night?

And with these thoughts and doubts, I trudged along the now flattening path as I descended again to the agricultural lands where men lived and villages turned the mud for food.

I was weary of my quest. I was weary of my supposed secret insights. And I was secretly fearful of that weird revelation that had struck me, that evening on the grey rock ledge, that I did not actually exist at all, and that all the shimmering beauty that I had dipped into was merely a meaningless weaving, winding procession of the inner and the outer, with no beginning and no end and no purpose.

And I was lonely and hungry

Chapter 6

The Grey Dog

*N*ow my daughters,

I think I shall tell you the story of the grey dog. If I

was to tell you the whole story and all that is to be

learned from this unhappy saga, I should take many

days. But I would not devote such energy to such a

fearful and regretful episode. For indeed for all I have

learned from that terrible time I would never choose

to go through it again, nor wish it upon another living

soul, if I had the power. And I fear that by even

giving breath to the story briefly, I have granted that

dog another evil pleasure and another chance to rob

me of the peace I claim is my deserving. And I would

not pass on to you a memory of an impure and terrible

thing for in my heart I can judge you two worthy of

only love and of peace. And though I have always

held that Truth justifies its own telling, I have

reluctantly come to believe that some Truths are so awful, that their telling should be, at the very least, brief in the extreme.

Yet if evil exists, I fear we must face it and overcome it. For though we have not chosen it as our companion in this life, we have found it here with us, and have no choice but to learn its nature and its ultimate undoing, for then, perhaps only then, shall we be free of its grasp. And perhaps in recounting this tale to you, though briefly, I shall arm you both against such evil as may seek to face you one day, and perhaps you shall more quickly achieve its undoing and become free yourselves, to enjoy that peace that is your birth-right.

And so I shall relate these events, though they spanned many years, in a few words.

After my wanderings in the mountains, I came upon a little city and resolved to spend my time there. I intended to offer my services to the good people of that place as An Architect. For though I had not completed my studies, I felt competent at my craft.

The Little City seemed at first a fairy-tale village. The sun shone with aggressive clarity upon the swishing grey waters of the lake-river. The wind blew from only two directions, East or West. Around the river were forests filled with a thousand different houses. Houses flowered like poems in a mind, or like flowers in a soft, stream-fed garden. Pine trees and cypress, acacia and flame-trees, even palm-trees by the river all grew without reserve. The white sand of the lake-side beach witnessed the games of girls and boys, and the meals of cormorants and seagulls. The city was crystalline and blue grey and confined to a shallow valley between a dark forest and the distant hills. Desert sands and wheat fields lay beyond the morning sunrise and tubular ocean waves were downstream at the river's end. Life seemed one of sweetness. In the white clouds flew gliders; real ones for the old men and toy ones for the young lads. Each headland into the river carried an important building: a University on one, a Kiosk on another, a Loony-Bin on one and an Hotel on another. The old jetty was grey wood. No-one remembered how it got there, but everyone loved to walk out and around on its sagging planks, which strummed like guitar strings as you walked on them.

But

Behind the blinding sunlight lurked every manner of evil, silent and smirking, treading lightly across the souls of men and leaving no footprints, yet with each soft trodden impression, laying a web of deceit, and of compromise, until a great invisible net was cast upon the souls of the city's inhabitants, and no-one paused to notice that anything was amiss.

Business men murdered each other, families tortured each other and lovers cheated each other. Disease and confusion ran through the town's walls like rats.

But I would assert then as still I do today, that the sure rhythm of the turning earth refuses to drop its vision. The blue earth is a young virgin. She is always unbegun. Only her parent's age. The world before her is old, she never is.

And so I stayed.

I found a job with a Warrior Man, who fashioned weapons for the city's soldiers. I worked steel and bone, brass and stone, fashioning shields and blades and hoping that they would be used only for noble purposes. I learned much at the Warrior Man's workshop, and my skill at working materials into well crafted and sturdy objects was much appreciated. My dreams of beauty and of objects of soaring inspiration were slowly forgotten as I settled into my new life.

Yet I was lonely, and the savage and cruel spirit of the city with a spear-sharp heart made me weep in the late night. I would swing gently from side to side in my rope hammock, under the dark verandah overhang at the back of the workshop where I lived.

Late one particularly dark night, I must have fallen into a deep sleep, for I had sudden, vivid dream. It was late in a long afternoon, as I lay reclined on the long couch in my long white house. Around about me the lazy cats slept, and the sun was still a long way from the horizon, when there came a knock at the door. Immediately I knew it was either a beautiful woman, or Death, but I knew not which. But the door had knocked and so I rose to open it…It was Death, a weak and sickly Death lacking in any pride or honour, complete with Grim-Reaper outfit and sickle. Death bade that I follow, so I obliged. I left my half finished meals, and my friends at their circular conversations by the window, and followed down the flag-stone path, past the playful letterbox to the sea shore. A wooden boat lay waiting, and the sun was setting, a fierce display of flaming red. I looked into the boat, two or three of my friends lay bound and gagged at the bottom.

As I stared in sickening terror, a sudden noise awoke me from the Dream. I heard snuffling and padded feet, knocking over bins in an apparently aimless night promenade. I turned curiously, awake now and pleased of the distraction from my grinding loneliness.

A great, lean grey dog was approaching. It was big, wiry, strong, and very, very ugly. I watched, with silent, intrigued absorption. Its wine-red eyes met mine and a trace of a smile flashed a warning across that hideous face.

I should have questioned that look, that inner knowing, that sarcastic cruelty. I have should have paused to reflect. But I held out my hand and said "Here little dog! Here my friend. Come and say hello!"

The great beast ambled leisurely towards me, as if only half interested. Alas I realised much later that the dog had sought me out, months before I even knew of its existence. It had even chased away a young stray cat I had befriended in order to secure my interest, and to remove any competition for my attention, and to intensify my loneliness. For indeed, one of the first things I was to discover about the great ridge-backed beast was its extra-ordinary intelligence.

In many ways it was more intelligent than men. Yes indeed.

And why had this great dog sought me out? Perhaps it too was lonely. Yet I think also it knew of my great skill in fashioning weapons, and it sought to make use of my skill in this regard. For this dog was a dog of war. It had teeth so long and yellow that one could but guess the deaths and wounds it had inflicted.

And how innocent was I that I suspected no such thing? I embraced this new found friend and spent my evenings and days off walking with it and tossing a branch for it to collect. We became as close friends. And even one night when the grey dog transformed, in a strange and almost imperceptible moment, into a great black beast, nearly double its original size, with an aurora of unmistakable evil, I only watched in innocent fascination and failed to heed the warning of that dark transfiguration. And indeed I delighted in its strength and irresistible power. And never in the months of that brief friendship did the savage men of that city seek to take advantage of me, for the dog was instantly at my side and threatening and snarling at those who would rob me or cheat me, or in other ways take advantage of my naivety. What a wonderful friend to have! Or so it seemed.

But that dog sought violence and vengeance with a lust that finally started to worry me. And it was only on the day that it started to tear strips of flesh from my own lower legs, after a small disagreement, with a strange rhythmic precision, that I started to fear the dark mind that was this beast's soul. Yet how could I abandon a friend? And so loyal a friend it had been.

I stood before the beast finally and said, "Oh Grey Dog, your violence appals me. No longer can I be your companion. Please leave me this day. But if you will, let us part in true friendship, and treasure always the loyalty and friendship that has been ours."

The dog responded with a low gurgling growl of disdain and said, "You are no better than all the rest. Look! You also have abandoned me! I shall leave, but I shall never truly leave. From this day I shall follow you as a shadow. And you shall never be free of me. And you shall never have another friend, for I shall kill every friend you seek, and destroy their families. And I shall follow you in the night and I shall undo every plan of your days. And you shall live to regret this decision of yours. Don't speak to me of friendship or loyalty. You are as bad as the rest. You shall know my power and you shall never again sleep a full night without terrible fear. You shall remember this warning and never be free of me! And if ever you seek to enlist help against me I shall vanish into the night and nobody will believe that I am real. They shall say you are mad and you are imagining things and never believe a word you utter, and still I will be there."

With that the dog disappeared into the night and I stood, trembling, but pleased at last to be alone. Let me not say too much of the terrible years that followed, but that the dog systematically carried out every last threat, and several deaths occurred at its terrible doing. Let me not count just how many years were wasted to this terrible and vengeful beast. Let me not describe in detail how I would awaken every night to the terrible snarling, or how many dear friends were terrified, not even knowing what had befallen them. Let me not describe the guilt I felt at being partially the cause of the spreading evil which persistently followed me and cruelly punished several innocent lives for the sake of hurting me. Let me not describe how many efforts of mine in the daylight hours were thwarted and undone by the clever and merciless guile of this beast. Let me not describe how

I pleaded and reasoned with the beast, forever believing that I would persuade it in the end, and it would see the virtue of compassion and forget its anger toward me.

And let me not describe the moment I finally abandoned the hope of reaching the dog with the conversion of love or of compassion and instead saw, at last, bitterly, that I was at war, and that as a Maker of Weapons, I too must at last learn to use them, and to use them with precision, though not with hate.

I will say only that after years of terror and despair, I began to take control of the situation. And I have come to believe that evil is an aberration, a small dark ripple on what is otherwise a vast, pure and luminous existence, whose majesty and goodness far out-weighs the illusory power of evil. Let me say only that I hold that evil is an aberration that the whole earth recognises and despises and whose time shall be finite. Let me say that evil appears to be large, just as an insect crawling across a window is momentarily mistaken for an enormous object in the distance, and that the calculation of the mind who first equated the size to something enormous, will duly realise that it is small, weak and that it will be crushed like a flea by a well-placed fingernail.

For on a journey into the desert some years later, I was suddenly struck by the vastness of the dry earth, and pondered the size and energy of the deep and rippling sands, and how free of the tricks of men the desert was and what power of purity must be stored, like the beating of a heart, in the orange earthen wilderness. And I prayed to the spirit of the vast earth to free me once and for all from the grey dog.

Later that same day, some Desert People stared at me, and their eyes seemed not the eyes of people but the very eyes of the earth itself. And they gave me a small hard green fruit to eat. After swallowing the tough thing, I felt briefly, but violently ill. I was later to learn that my friends at the same moment felt the same passing nausea and weakness.

And the terrible grey dog vanished and its influence was no longer felt. And I would conclude that every weapon in the world swung and thrust against the manoeuvring of evil is not enduringly effective though it be well meaning in its fight. But by contrast, when the very sands of the earth and the heartbeat of the ground beneath your feet is enjoined to banish evil, then evil has no chance and good will prevail.

My two daughters, I hope I have not frightened nor sickened you by relating this tale. For indeed I have feared its telling myself. But if I, and perhaps you, are to be truly free of what befell me, then I must needs pass that way without fear and tonight, perhaps,

I have done that. I love you both

Chapter 7

New Skills

$\mathcal{M}$y reputation preceded me like the whispering tide.
I became known as one of both skill, in handling the implements of war, and of compassion. On occasions people would approach me with unusual requests, and I would often attempt new and unusual tasks. I had still not turned my hand to making tables and chairs, and though I occasionally pondered it, I had not resumed my pursuit of the creation of objects of beauty.

On occasions I would take my chisels when requested, and remove thorns from the hooves of horses. I once removed a splinter of bone from the gums of a lion. I strapped a splint to the broken leg of an elephant and assisted it to heal straight and true. I even sewed a new cloak of feathers for a pelican with a damaged wing. And I say to you, as I watched the great black and white bird skim the silver waters of the lake on his new wings, I marvelled at his grace, and dismissed the notion that objects of stone and wood could ever be capable of matching such beauty.

One day word was sent to me of a new and strange task, demanding my attention. It was rumoured that a small fishing village hundreds of miles down the coast had sought my services. The oysters in the sea were apparently, mysteriously ill

.

Chapter 8

A Deep Sea Oyster Surgeon

S atyina and Angelica. How are you both?
Shall I continue with my story? Yes? I am glad you
weren't scared. You are both so beautiful. You have
more grace than women, more strength than men and
deeper wisdom than even the Gurus of the Indus. I
am grateful and awed by your love. I shall tell you
more. For now I am coming to the bit about how I
came to be engaged in the Work I now do, and indeed
why tonight I must say goodbye to you both for
another while. And whilst I am gone, you shall know
why, and you shall know what it is that I am doing,
far below these forested mountain valleys, and further
below, beneath the waves of the purple sea.

I gladly left the Little City and journeyed by foot
down the coast to the Fishing Village. I carried with

me just a small bag of tools. As I approached the village, the land beside the sea became steeper and more overgrown. Great jungles advanced away up the slopes into steaming clouds that hung all day like the steam from a kettle. The village itself nestled in a tiny, tight, white-pebbled cove, surrounded on all sides by these towering jungled cliffs. Great mossy branches and immense feathered leaves overhung the village like curtains, or like the hair of a weeping woman. Occasionally during the time I spent in the village, I would ask the people about the mountains, and what lay further above, beyond the mist. They always replied, slightly surprised at my question, that nothing lay further up, beyond the mist. The mist they said was proof that there was nothing beyond, because, they explained, it was because of the mist that nothing could be seen beyond.

Certainly their arguments were logical, and these people prided themselves on their logical, common sense ways. However, the more I thought about their reply, the less it made sense to me. And indeed my daughters, the truth is that those mountains, are these. The jungled cliffs that those good people dismissed, are the foothills of these very mountains in which we live. And it is the fact of their always looking to the sea, that they have not suspected the pure air and lovely forests that we three call home. And that is why, in a world peopled in every land and in every place in every land, these mountains alone remain unknown and unvisited. To a people who say what cannot be seen cannot exist, these wonderful flower-jewelled fields and peaks would seem only an imagining, if someone with more patience than I should try and tell them.

Why don't I tell them Satyina? Why don't I? My daughter, Child of my flesh, because I am weary. For it was these same people who were to ridicule me for another claim I was to make shortly after my arrival at their little village. And their ridicule was cruel, and I have not the desire left in my bones to convince anyone of anything, though in my heart I know I have knowledge and experience that falls infinitely beyond the imagining of men. My daughters, what happened is this.

I arrived at the village at nightfall, or shortly after. It was all I could do to find a small Guest-house to rest for the night. The following morning I found my way to the head-man of the village and introduced myself. He confirmed that he had called for me and explained why.

"Word has been received", he said "from certain fish in the region, that the oysters in the next bay are seriously ill. And though we ourselves do not fish these oysters, or very rarely, we understand that the health of the sea depends on the health of all that is in it."

And indeed if there be one virtue of the peoples of this time, it is their profound understanding of the inter-dependence of all life. Though it is scarcely believable, that there was a peoples who populated this world before us, in unknown civilisations of ages past, who removed entire forests from the face of the earth, Imagine that! Destroyed forests and let grass take their place.

There is of course the well known legend of the Un-Developer. The Un-Developer, it is said, was the most wealthy man in the Great Southland. He was immensely wealthy. No-one was more wealthy than he, or very few perhaps. And he journeyed through the Great City of the Southland. For in the whole continent, which is vast, there was only one city, but an immense one. The City stretched almost the entire way around the coast of the continent, without break or interruption. It was immense. It stretched the full length of the East coast and turned the corner at the South and stretched the full length of the South coast, turned the corner again and stretched the full length of the West coast. Only a short stretch along the North was without the great shiny buildings of these people. And the Un-Developer began his strange path of destruction on the East coast, in the area known since times long forgotten as the Gold Coast. He bought large districts of the most valuable buildings, hundreds of them.....and demolished them. He replaced them with every type of living thing; trees, flowers, animals which people thought no longer existed. And with great care and attention to detail he proceeded around the coast of the mighty continent, in his quest for destruction. And he destroyed vast distances of the Great City. Progressively, without remorse or regret, he systematically destroyed the entire city which had been there for countless ages past, nobody knows how long, probably since time began. And he replaced the whole thing with forests, and woodlands, and wetlands and every type of place. And no two places he created were alike. Each was distinctly different, and richly varied. If indeed the legend is true, then perhaps that is the origin of the current understanding. Or perhaps it is only a legend, invented to explain the strict laws under which we all now live and nurture every living thing.

In any case, the Head Man of the fishing village had explained himself to me, and I understood well his concern for the illness of the shellfish, that perhaps even he, had never seen.

I asked him how I was to get to the bay, as the village was isolated by the awesome cliffs and the rocky point seemed equally un-traversable. He directed me to the boat yard and instructed me to learn to paddle one of their boats.

Those boats were something else! I had never seen anything so primitive. They were constructed of three large, roughly squared logs, sewn together with rope, side by side. The prow of the boat was fashioned equally simply from three, tapered smaller pieces, also sewn in place, by a few rough, thick ropes. By virtue of the taper in the three bow-pieces they ascended in a sort of a point, and this simple device allowed the boat to punch through the waves without being swamped. The whole design was so simple, I was astounded that something so primitive was still in use. It was like a piece of ancient history, thrown into the present. Try as I may, I could not paddle the wretched thing. It was heavy and unwieldy. Those three squared logs were a cumbersome and antiquated trinity, though not without a certain charm.

If I was to fulfil my commission and make it to the next bay, I would have to fashion a craft of my own design, something a little more easily managed.

Something simpler, lighter, smaller

.

Chapter 9

Something Simpler, Lighter, Smaller

A fter several false starts, I arrived at a design. It used just one squared log instead of three. It was just half the length of their craft and the log was pared away to a far more slender blade of timber. I curved it like a leaf, tapered at both ends, and no thicker than your wrist at its thickest point. It was light to carry and smooth to the touch. Being shaped from a single timber it had no need of clumsy sewing. The prow was carved in a gentle upward curve, enabling it to be paddled through the waves, just as the clumsy three piece prow of their own design had intended. I had drawn upon my memory of those ink-line drawings the visiting Teacher at the School of the Makers of Architecture, all those years ago. For indeed it seems to me that the most beautiful things of this world are not beautiful without reason. And though I have heard many bitter and envious voices deride the beauty of some beautiful women, I have never found a woman beautiful who was not also possessed of a deep and graceful inner poise. And I dispute any claims that beauty is an ephemeral and irrelevant attribute, be it in reference to the face of a man, the eyes of a woman, the form of a carved item of furniture, or the sweep of trees across the tumbling folds of a valley. And the boat that I fashioned was scarcely more than a board, yet it had a grace and a simplicity of curve, like a hand, held relaxed, and ready. For I was soon to discover the remarkable performance that my board was capable of, and it was in no small measure by virtue of its wonderfully wrought shape.

It took me some many months to learn to master even this modest vessel, but master it I did. During the course of my work, I would paddle the board out into the bay, lying on my belly and paddling with my hands, one on either side of the board. I rounded the point, going wide to avoid being washed onto the rocks and came into the second bay. The second bay was a vast, radiant white blade of sand, virgin white, untrodden by the feet of men and warm in the sun that poured from the sky, unobstructed by any towering peaks on that side.

It was necessary to come ashore to rest and prepare myself for the next stage, which was to dive to the secret oyster beds, of which I had been told. However coming ashore was no simple matter. For the ocean swells, so even and rolling in the deep water of the open sea, transformed themselves into shattered, howling monsters as they reached the radiant white shoreline, and as they passed over the concealed sand banks that lay below the surface for the full length and depth of the bay. The bay itself was not curved as one imagines a bay to be. It was straight like the blade of a sword.

Do you know how I make it to the shore, in that violent battle field of peeling waves? I sit astride my board, just outside the line of the breaking waves and await, with great patience, the advance of the procession of ocean waves. They advance in sets at spaced intervals, spaced within the sets, and spaced between them. It is like some cosmic play of rhythms of vast scale, a heart beat that originates in the bosom of the Universe herself. And as you await their patient advance, bright blue in the brilliant sun, you learn their shapes and their patterns of motion: how quickly they peel, whether they peel left or right, or straight down. Every day is different, and every hour of every day is different. And those occasional days that a light offshore breeze is blowing, the waves are hollowed out like the smooth skin of a young woman's stomach, in a gentle and lovely form and they peel in travelling tubes, aquamarine, momentary jewelled objects of infinite beauty. Three dimensional forms peeling and transforming in the fourth dimension of time, the ultimate sculpture, the ultimate poem written in water.

If such beauty could be worn about a woman's neck, she would be the most desirable lady in the land. And yet much beauty can only be gazed at. Not waves. The exact form and glassy light beauty that delights the eye may also be embraced by a person on a board such as mine, and the driving thrusting flow of the liquid surface becomes a dance, an arcing, pulling, turning poem in movement, silent, fast and powerful. A gift of speed and motion to the souls of men, from the Ocean herself... A dance, the curling, whirling dance of the surfy. A copulation of purity and of eternal youth. A gift of silence and ecstasy. You drive with your legs, you pivot with your hips, you lean against the shifting invisible weight of your momentum and cast your arms wide as you adjust your balance against the constantly transforming revelation of the waves' purpose.

The moment of paddling into the titling face of the wave is critical, and the sudden acceleration of the smooth board down the face of the wave is the signal to pounce to your feet in a good strong stance.

Then the ride is yours, all the way to the warm dry sand.

Will I ever forget those late golden evenings, when the sun was so low that it lit up the glass tube from behind, the light scattered through the turning water, and engulfed me in a dancing, cascading, liquid chandelier of golden yellow light, as I sped down the line

Chapter 10

A Disturbing Discovery

*H*aving reached the second bay, the hard work begins.

It became necessary to learn to hold my breath for an entire day, in order to dive deep enough, and remain long enough, to attend to my work in the oyster beds. This took much training, and is one of the reasons for my unusually large chest. But having mastered the ability, I could dive downwards, like a bird flying, to the place where the oysters cluster on the submerged reef.

And so I began my investigations into the plight of the oysters. It was no easy task. An oyster is a small, gnarled grey shell fish, who clutches the crevices of reefs and clings against the pouring and returning of the ocean's tides. They are very quiet animals who speak very little. Though each oyster is quite unique, they are nevertheless quite difficult to tell apart. And I could detect no indication as to which were ill and which were healthy.

I started to prise at their little shells with my finer tools, poking and levering. To each oyster as I approached I would say, "Say Aaughh!" And if I was quick, and if I was delicate in my touch, I could take a peek inside their shells as they opened just a crack and have a look around. I would shine my tiny surgical torch at the moist, smooth grey flesh, looking for any sign of anything out of the ordinary.

I could find nothing, and furthermore, each oyster would sometimes mutter, "No, not me, silly, I am a healthy oyster. I know there are one or two ill ones, but I am not they. I am healthy". And before I could quiz them further, the shy little creatures would snap shut their lids and utter not one single word more.

And I was left in the dark, literally, and indeed was left in the cold and the damp, for the Ocean is, if nothing else, very, very damp.

Oh the frustration of my search! Day after day, week after week, the same fruitless search, until I started to doubt that indeed there was anything behind the claim that brought me here in the first place.

Each night I would light a fire on the silky white sand in the shelter behind a large rock, only yards from the sweeping wash of the night waves. I would crouch, warm and comfortable behind the rock and feed pieces of driftwood and dry branches into its golden flames. I would cook fresh fish, caught that very evening, and fry it in a little oil with a sprinkling of herbs. Never has the meat of fish tasted so sweet. And I would cook bread in the white coals of the late evening fire, and it was steaming and soft, and moist and white. And I would make a black brew of tea.

They were wonderful, lovely evenings. The music, perpetually playing throughout the days and nights, was the screaming roar of the sea. It never ceased and never silenced.

I would sleep on the low sand dunes themselves, just behind a low shrub, out of the wind, and fall asleep gazing at the vast and infinite black star lit universe. I could see not a thing other than that vast field of stars. The soft sand, beneath my body supported me gently, and it felt for all the world that I was floating in that oceanic universe. Perhaps indeed we are.

Of course living was tough in the wilderness like that, and it was important to find enough water each day, and to be watchful of the enormous venomous snakes that lived just beyond the dunes in the tangled undergrowth. And the shoreline itself is a graveyard of creatures who have succumbed to the violence of the ocean. One felt, at times, very small and vulnerable in the wild coastal wilderness there. Those poets and painters who have glorified the play of dolphins and the wonders of the sea, sometimes seem to me a little removed from the objects of their admiration, and do not fully comprehend the violence of their subject. Whales were not infrequently washed ashore to die slow deaths on dry land, claiming ignorance of the illegality of trafficking scrimshaw.

One night, as I kept watch beside my little fire, I started to hum a little tune. As I became aware of my own humming, I tried to place the tune, and guess what song it was that I was humming. I could not place it. Suddenly I realised that it as a new tune, one that had come to me, fresh from the night. I started to put words to the tune and made up a little song about the Second Bay. A little song about the place in which I was camped.

Oh no Angelica, I can't sing it now!

No 'please's', No!

Oh…………all right. Ahem:

The Wildest Coast of All your Dreams

Has punctured paltry porpoise themes

And whales impaled on shifting sand

Are left to ponder contraband.

Let only those with four foot beards

Contemplate this scenery weird

You who pass here, Take the trip

Drop your pack and catch a ship,

For n'ere before was such at stake:

Dying of thirst and stung by snake.

Remember me as one not lost

But frozen dead in midnight frost.

I was camped on that beach for nearly a year. I

continued my search, with gradually dwindling hope.

I began to feel that I may have been misled. Indeed I was starting to plan to leave this place and to leave the little fishing village, when I made a disturbing discovery. It was the end of another day's diving. I had tapped on the little shells, and poked and pried. I had inquired and searched for some sign of the illness that I had been sent to deal with. I was preparing to return to the surface and to get dry and warm, when it happened.

It was six in the evening. The sun was getting low; you can tell this even below the surface because the wonderful golden evening light slips below the surface at such a low angle that the rocky caves are all lit up, brightly, as if illuminated each from within. You can see all the fish, and other strange creatures in that lovely golden glow, that last twenty minutes before night falls. I was turning to look upwards, back to the wobbling, shimmering surface of the sea above me, preparing to make my ascent back to the air, when a slight movement caught my eye, just beside and below me. A small unremarkable oyster was slowly opening its shell, and that golden evening light lit its delicate flesh. I nearly gasped a lung full of water. For there in the gently trembling lip of the little animal was something that did not belong. It was not a splinter and it was not a thorn. It was not a sting, nor a fisherman's hook. It was like nothing I had ever seen before. Utterly unlike anything I had ever seen. It glowed with a gentle silvery white light. It was small and perfectly round, more round than the very earth that sailors have bound up in the criss-crossing paths of their voyages.

The object was pure and luminous. It was perfect and flawless. It absorbed my gaze and became as a thing of vastness, an immense new field of light and glory. Something utterly without compare in the entire universe of experience. A fathomless, unfolding, infinite, and glorious new realm of splendour and beauty. No words shall ever describe the perfection, nor the awesome beauty, power and infinite, rippling silence. And it was the more remarkable for it so perfectly fit the descriptions I had heard in legends of old, which have all since been discarded as crazed imaginings by the more common sense people of today. Yet it could be nothing else. Its reality was manifest and unambiguous. It clearly was, exactly what it was. And no invented alternative explanation would ever suffice, for it was none other than a Pearl

Chapter 11

The Pearl

*H*ave you ever wondered how a single thing could be every other thing? And at the same time far beyond their reach? Have you ever wondered if all that we know and experience, though apparently complete may in some way be an illusion, a trick of the mind, and that there may be beyond all this, a vaster existence and more infinite sense of being?

Have you ever wondered if amidst the weakness and ugliness of our fleshly existence, there may be something that is anchored in light, in the Eternal, in the unchanging mysteries that soar beyond our imaginings? Have you ever wondered just exactly how white light can be said to contain every other hue of the rainbow and yet still be white? Has that assertion sometimes not seemed a little too fabulous to believe?

But, as I gazed at the vast new vista of light and beauty revealed by the Pearl, I saw all these things. The modest grey beast, in all its weakness and vulnerability, had spun this jewel from its very flesh. A tumour of a crystalline purity, that answered the irritation of some foreign object lodged, without invitation, in the weak and quivering flesh of the poor creature's body. A response to an unfortunate circumstance that transformed an illness into a majestic accomplishment of light, wonder and exquisite silence.

And in one blinding, irreversible and overwhelming fracture, a new and vaster vision vaporised that earlier awful apparition, that had appeared before me on the grey rock ledge, all those months ago:

Where I had come face to face with a reality in which no depth, no matter how deep, or subtle, or personal was mine, my own, separate, sanctified, apart from the entirety of the Universe;

Where-by I had formulated myself out of existence;

Where-by the existence of each of us as individuals appeared to be an illusion;

Whereby the Whole was a self-sufficient mechanical unity; and "I am" was not any part of it.

How could white light be said to contain every other hue of the rainbow and yet still be white? The Pearl, with infinite gentleness and clarity unmasked all that had yet been hidden.

But what is true is always true. And the truth of the earlier awful vision remained, though now utterly transformed;

"I am" is not of this world, "I am" is far beyond its vaporous reach.

"I am"

Is:

None of it,

And all of it,

And much more besides.

This much may I say, without committing offence. Beyond this I would declare things I cannot verify.

And the soft white light of the Pearl revealed and recalled every other hue as I gazed at it. It was rich with the shifting shades of ocean - pink and sunset - green, mauves and blues so gentle and iridescent that they had not comparison in any other thing on this earth. And the colours, though infinite in their variety, were not like the obvious and much loved ribbon of colour that all call a rainbow. They were more varied than the colours of the rainbow, but far more subtle, far softer. And as you turned your gaze to contemplate one particular shifting hue, it seemed to vanish and to become some other, and the whole time you were perfectly aware that you were gazing in fact, at an object more white, more purely white than the white of the snow on the peaks outside our house. If Emptiness could indeed be Fullness, if the Simplest could indeed be the Richest and most complex, if the most modest in form and appearance could indeed be the most grand and the most sumptuous, then the Pearl was the proof.

And a strange irony dawned upon me, that my original quest, when I stole away from the School of the Makers of Architecture, all those years ago, had been to seek to uncover the secret forms of beauty that would take away people's breath and awe them in wonder at the majesty of beauty in this existence. And by a strange unravelling of events, my path had led me to precisely that objective, in a most unplanned and unintended manner, via the most seemingly unlikely route, which had brought me through the fields of weapons and war, compassion and healing, and loneliness and isolation. And here, at last, before me, was an object, not of my own design or making, but certainly of my own discovery, that far exceeded the paltry imaginings of all my years of efforts in this field.

I gazed in wonder at the Pearl.

Then as I became aware of the dimming of the evening light, I reached gently forward with my finest blade, and deftly scooped the thing from the cupped flesh of the Oyster, who breathed a sigh of relief at its removal, thanked me meekly and quickly closed its shell against the cold of the ocean currents.

Some day for somebody like me!

Some are deceived by the apparent finiteness of this world.

Some are delighted by the proofs of another.

Some are they: fortunate but very, very few to whom ancient and discarded myths are proven more Real than the apparent reality of ordinary life.

Some day!

Coming ashore at last, I dropped to the silk sand to rest. The steel blue ocean tore at the beach, in a slow agonising cry of loneliness. The sun had probably set but there was no way of knowing. The sky was thick with warm clouds as a cyclone prowled the coast, eyeing the shoreline for an entry. The sand was decorated with intricate floral designs, marbles of sand flung like petals from the small central hole of a burrowing crab: scattered embroidery like a lace and pearl wedding dress. Between them were many tangled, aimless scribblings starting and finishing nowhere, some lost sea snail searching the sea as the tide raced back to the horizon. As I gazed up the thin white sandy line of the infinite shoreline, a strange trepidation overtook me. For all that I now knew, what had I really gained? How, if at all, was I changed?

If I walk to the very end of this beach and back, I mused,

I'll have got no where,

but I'll Know Where,

I now am.

A faint pink polygon appeared briefly, close to the horizon, like a glance as a door is held open just a moment longer, before a beloved leaves. "Remember what I told you," it seemed to say, a stern glance held a moment longer than necessary, with the implicit trust of a friend.

How good it is to be loved by the very Universe.

As I gazed about me, at the now breathtakingly
beautiful reality of this earth, the sea, the white sand;
my finger started to write, a spontaneous expression
of the heart, not so much a prayer, as of prayerfulness.
My hand wrote:

Tonight I made love with a girl called Silence

We swam in a similar sea

For one perfect hour as our bodies met

The world was unwrapped for me

And every beating body cell

And every shaking nerve

Was met and matched, and laid in peace

As curve enfolded curve.

Desire opens bleeding wounds

And thirst breaks open flesh

But Silence calmly healed the whole

Made good the tearing mesh.

And pregnant with fulfilled desire

And pregnant with restraint

She met and matched a whole life's woes

and smoothed away all taint.

Pausing, I then wrote several more words, which are secret. Then the rushing sea reclaimed my scrawl.

I fashioned a rough bracelet for myself from a piece of blue rope and a tiny pink cuttlefish, each delivered to my feet by two successive waves, which washed the hand written prayer from the sands at my feet; A gift of friendship, a promise made to my soul by the sea herself.

A lone sand piper scurried anxiously about the exposed shoreline, seeking refuge from the cyclone out at sea, a world wide migration cut short as a hardy band of fellow, feathered souls scattered, a fate interrupted and an annual ritual rocked out of its eternal rhythm. Danger was implicit in the long exhalation, that was the on-shore wind. Nobody felt safe.

Then as night spread about the luminous grey sky, I was enfolded by light, not darkness, and I knew the heart of every paradox; Man is wild and wildness is beauty. A deeper rhythm owns our spirits. There is but one Law, and it is nameless

Chapter 12

The Annunciation

I n the days that followed, I came to recognise the tell tale signs;

Signs that indicated the presence of this illness in the individual oysters of the sea. And it was only one more month before I had identified, I believe, most of the oysters thus suffering in the bay and had removed the source of their irritation. In all there were about one dozen of the poor creatures, and I removed from each, a pearl no less beautiful than the first. They varied in size, but not in perfection. I wrapped them in a broad soft leaf that I gathered from the woodlands behind the beach and folded it carefully.

It was time then to return to the village and present my findings to the Head Man of the village, and collect my pay. I tucked the folded leaf of pearls into my pants and paddled my board back out and around the point to the dark steamy valley of the fishing village.

"Oh here he is!", the people exclaimed as I walked slowly back up the muddy streets of the village. "We thought you must have got lost!" the people said, " Or just gone home without even telling us!"

I smiled a shy smile and shook my head. It had been such a long time since I had seen any people and I was uncertain around them. "What kept you?" I heard some one say. "Fraud!" I heard some one mutter below their breath, quite close behind me, I turned but no-one met my gaze. I was starting to feel uneasy.

I came to the home of the Head Man. He looked up from his coffee, a little surprised and a little annoyed. He said nothing but held his eyebrows arched and waited for me to speak. He was wearing a big blue shirt, and seemed himself, smaller and older than I remembered him in the year ago since I first met him.

"Good Sir", I began. "The task was difficult, as I was at first unfamiliar with the creatures of the sea, but I duly ascertained the cause of the illness of the oysters and I have operated on every last one of them and I am happy to report that they are now all well."

He silently handed me one black coin, carved from the shell of an unknown type of sea-shell and turned back to his companions, ignoring me.

"Sir" I continued, "One thing more…"
He turned slowly back to me and met my eyes, in an accusing, sceptical sort of way.
"I have discovered, in the course of my work, the Pearl."

The Head Man slouched and laughed, gazing at his shaking cup of coffee, chuckling self indulgently to himself, until finally lifting his gaze, holding my eyes for a moment and repeated,

"A Pearl?" He chuckled again, and his companions joined in the merriment.

"Yes Sir", I replied and I should like to give it to you for a fair but modest exchange, before leaving your Village by the Sea.

"You would?" he asked, in a manner that seemed as though he was humouring me.

"Yes Sir, " I replied, "It is a real, glorious, beautiful Pearl from the bottom of the Sea. A jewel more valuable than a diamond, and more mysterious, being as it is fashioned in the bosom of a living thing."

"You have been in the sun too long boy." He said with a twisted little smile, "Or having you been drinking sea water hmmmm? Everybody knows that pearls are the subject of legends. They were made up to entertain simple people in the dull darkness of the night. There is no such thing as a pearl, and there never has been. I have never met anyone quite so naive as your poor self." He said.

I grew grave as I realised that my claims were not being taken seriously. How could they not take me seriously? Was not my very manner proof enough of my claims? Did they take me for a liar? A trickster? I was insulted, but confused as to what I should say in response. It had never occurred to me in all the time I had prepared for my return, that anyone would doubt what I had to tell them, and I was thus unprepared to counter their insulting rejections. I was lost for words.

I know the thought that has written its self across your brow Satyina. You wonder why I did not simply show the Head Man a Pearl. It is not such a mystery. Those who cannot abide possibilities outside their own belief, will not believe what is thrust under their nose, no matter how Real or Manifest it may be, and a grave wrong is committed to so violate so precious a Truth.

To him who prides himself on Scepticism, and who confuses scepticism with rationality, the path to education is too laborious to attempt. How can they be made to see that scepticism is more prejudicial to understanding the possibilities of Truth and of Reality, than is the apparent naivety of Innocence. Sceptics deny possibility, without offering any justification for so doing. The truth is that such are cowards, and fear what may be.

Such a one will not even allow that, that which exists, do so, though it already exist. I would leave each to their own; the sky is no place for such as these, yet a man is forbidden wings, long after he has grown them!

Science demands that we investigate with an open mind every possibility that Reality throw before us. Yet it is those mediocre men who claim to be champions of science who in fact exercise the least discipline, in maintaining open enquiry, where the truth of more profound matters is concerned.

Truly no man is more naive than the sceptic. Would that this be my offering. Should my entire story unravel and be blown away by the wind, let that one thought remain as my eternal challenge to the intelligent. No man is more naive than the sceptic.

Satyina, Any thing I could show would have been dismissed as forgery. The matter is that simple.

Word quickly spread around the village and soon wry smiles and laughter greeted me wherever I walked. I was ostracised by lunchtime, and threatened by teatime.

The Head Man cornered me later that evening, shaking with anger, as if by uttering my outrageous claims in his presence, I had somehow tarnished his own credibility before the people of the village and he now went all out to restore his pride by humiliating me. "No one will ever tell me, in my own village!" he yelled, "what Is and what Is Not. And you have no right to assume that I don't have my own opinion about the subject of pearls. I am a man of the sea and I know better than you what is and what is not! You have a lot of nerve to go about telling me what I should and should not know!"

Oh my daughters! Is there any suffering like that of a soul ostracised and rejected by both the highest and the lowest of the society in which he must dwell? How is it that when a few take on a view, the rest follow without any direct information for themselves about the truth of a matter? Why is it that to be rejected by a few equates automatically to rejection by all?

I have heard people speak with derision of sheep, and who say that they follow the flock without a thought of their own. And I have heard people who speak in derision of dogs, who say they are savage and merciless when they get the scent of blood. But I say unto you, that humankind thinks less than any sheep before following, and tears more savagely at the flesh of an abandoned soul than any dog, and I despair at the stupidity and the cruelty of humankind. The tiger is not so savage, and no other creature so stupid. And before long untrue stories were invented by the people to augment the already fantastic (though entirely true) claim I had made. My very name provoked laughter.

And it seems to be true that a Prophet is indeed accepted in every land and by every peoples but by his own. And it seems incredible that this audacious claim can still hold true so many millennia after its author first uttered it. Slowly but surely, I became an object of fun, a buffoon, an amusing fool. Why did I accept this identity, this role? Well, I didn't really. But I was offered no other. Are you not aware that the name you are known by is not a name chosen by yourself, but one given to you by others? And so it is that I became their fool. An identity not of my choosing.

My dear ones. As soon as I was able, I left that village with a heavy heart and set off with the resolve to find one who would recognise the simple truth of my modest claims. For it seemed proper that having discovered the truth of the old legend of Pearls, that I should make it known and perhaps receive some small and modest recompense for my discovery. The beauty of these oceanic jewels alone surely merited some small recompense. And surely some others would be happy to be given the opportunity to acquire these beautiful gifts of the sea.

Chapter 13

The Man Who Is Like A Hole in

The Sky

I made it my business to research all the old scrolls concerning divers.

And I sought to ascertain whether any other living soul may also know of, and value this rare and wonderful diamond of the Deep. It was not so hard to find accounts of times long past, but reports of contemporary Pearls proved very rare indeed. Some of the accounts appeared fraudulent, though it was impossible to tell. I was in no mind to travel immense distances to be confronted with a trickster, when the matter was so real to me and so important. I jotted down a couple of names of famous divers, some of whom spoke of Pearls, and some of whom didn't. I weighed carefully their words, their manner, the hand drawn line drawings of their faces, trying to decide of I could trust any of them.

One man stood out. He appeared unremarkable enough in the drawings but many strange and wonderful tales related to him. One tale concerning him said that this particular diver was not a diver at all, but a man born at the deepest depth of the Ocean, who only after his birth came to the shore we all call home. I reserved my judgement on this particular claim, and set off to see him, with my small treasure tucked, in its leaf wrapper, under my hessian cloak.

The man from the deep lived in The Land Where Two Seas Meet. I travelled there in a white Glider. I will not say much about him tonight, though at some later time I may say more. But when I saw him walking slowly and gracefully about the garden in front of his modest cottage, I was awe-struck by his grace and a strange luminous presence that seemed to accompany him. Senses beyond the usual five, tingled and stretched, straining to pin down a feeling that something incredible was before me. Yet my eyes and ears could report nothing extraordinary, and such other senses as would be necessary to verify these matters are not mine to enjoy. So I glimpsed in an imperfect and momentary way the power and majesty of this fellow, and felt immediately that here was one who knew not only of my Pearls but of other riches yet unspoken. He was, in the immensity of his majesty, like a Hole in the Sky, a window on a grander fact of our being, a gift to us by his mere presence.

He received my gift of one dozen Pearls in silence and held my gaze for a long, wordless and intimate moment. In that minute I knew his power and his knowledge and his wisdom. My hurts at the insults I had endured melted away in the knowledge my precious find was now in the hands of one who knew their value and their authenticity.

I turned silently and reluctantly to leave his cottage and his loyal attendants delivered hampers of gifts to me in exchange for the gift I had given the Man Who Is Like a Hole in The Sky. And in the hampers were many small and unusual things, and each was something that I needed most desperately. There were herbs for medicine, small scrolls of knowledge, unusual tools to help me in my work and gifts of sweets and flutes. But He gave me, above all else, acceptance. He had anointed me with acknowledgment, and crowned me with clear assurance that I was not mad, and never had been, and he put the world beneath my feet. All this he did with a long, silent, fierce glance, and I wept.

The last thing that happened before I turned and left his garden was this: A small white rose bush grew by his gate. Some of the flowers were fully opened and their petals, backlit by a setting sun, glowed luminous. I wondered at the countless petals that made up each flower. Like the souls of this earth, each one was separate and lived alone and fell alone when each their time was done.

Then out of the corner of my eye I spied a single fresh white rosebud, an unopened bud. It lay partly concealed within the green foliage, compact and round, itself exactly like a pearl, white and soft as snow, moist as new love. Infinitely delicate, this living jewel now caught my gaze and would not allow me to turn away. Within the curve of the single outer petal of that rosebud lay wrapped the entirety of the whole flower. All that the flower was, lay within the enfolding cup of that single petal. And I saw that within the rosebud three apparently irreconcilable truths coexisted in perfect balance: Every petal was completely individual; yet every petal sprang from and depended upon a single common source, a "beyond", the green stem; And thirdly, as impossible as it seemed, the whole flower was contained *within* each single petal.

The impossible vision of the pearl was explained by its gentle sister, the rose. And since then I have ceased to be troubled by the inexplicable. I am now comfortable with mystery and content to reside within my simple being.

I am - and that is enough.

My dear sweet ones. I think perhaps I have told you everything now that was weighing in my heart to tell. I could not part before the dawn without sharing something of my Work with you. Perhaps you will understand, and abide more patiently for my return, now that I have shared these things with you both.

For in my Heart there is now a peace that I have taken you into the confidence of my Heart. For if I had not taken you into the confidence of my Heart, how could I call myself your Father? Come now, stretch those legs and we shall tuck you into your bright bed. Here we go, one under each arm, you wriggly little things...Ouch

Chapter 14

Two Kisses

S leep well my two dear ones. I shall not be gone so long.
The cow will always give you milk and the cupboards are full. Dream bright and happy dreams. A kiss for you Angelica.   And a kiss for you Satyina.
Goodnight!

Chapter 15

Dawn

Angela finally noticed that she was shivering violently, in the pre-dawn, mid-winter cold. A cacophony of shrieking, from thousands of tiny birds, heralded the last hour of darkness. She saw a shy pink dawn approach with disregard. Then night fled to the West like a startled dog, sideways, blue and skulking. Through the loose foliage of the stand of eucalypts at the bottom of her garden, and down beyond the rise of the hill on which her cottage stood, she could see the serene, luminous white sheet of the broad expanse of the river. The first traffic of the peak hour was already rushing to insane destinations. The early morning freeway stream of coloured metal flowed beside the placid river, a live rattling necklace.

She noticed an unusually large bird circling overhead. As she watched she realised it was an osprey, unusual these days. It seemed to be circling directly over their house. She wondered where its nest must be.

She turned toward the house. She knew what she had to do. She picked up the receiver of the black telephone and dialled directory inquiries. She was going to find her father. "Hello?" she said, a little croaky, and probably coming down with a cold, "Yes I am trying to find a phone number...... No I don't know which city, I'm not even sure of the country....the name? Reese Carnegie". A magpie sang and the golden yellow sun devoured the early dawn.

The End

www.ingramcontent.com/pod-product-compliance
Lightning Source LLC
Chambersburg PA
CBHW071451070426
42452CB00039B/1029